Dreams

Jennifer Ollie

Copyright © 2024 A Written Dream, LLC

Published by: Writers Publishing House

Paperback ISBN: 978-1-64873-522-6

All rights reserved. No part of this book may be reproduced in any manner whatsoever without written permission from the author except in the case of brief quotations embodied in critical articles and reviews.

Dreams

A Collection of Love Poems

Jennifer Ollie

Writers Publishing House

I would like to dedicate this collection of poetry to anyone out there who has ever loved, healed and pursued their dreams even during some of life's most challenging moments.

Author's Note

True dreams are what keeps us up at night. They feel like the rhythm of life that keeps beating, an intangible item that we yearn to make us feel whole and purposeful. At times, dreams feel like the fabric of vulnerability, love and remaining hopeful for the days ahead. Thank you in advance for dreaming with me...

Contents

Magnets.... 1
OK.... 2
The Climb.... 3
Still.... 4
I Miss You.... 7
The Wait.... 8
Beyond the Stars.... 9
Needed.... 10
The Memory.... 14
Nice Things.... 16
Background.... 19
Solitude (pt. 1).... 20
Solitude (pt. 2).... 21
The Reach.... 23
Tomorrow.... 24
Blooming.... 27
Fresh Start, v. 1.... 28
Fresh Start, v. 2.... 29
Moving On.... 30
The Wait.... 32
The Colors of Love.... 33
Paradise.... 36
Remembering You.... 37
Good Love.... 38

Magnets

We are magnets
Unattached
Moving through life apart but intuitively connected
We are magnets
Bonded by the force of love
Words unspoken
Walking home alone
We are deeply rooted
Undeniably we fit
Because we are magnets

OK

The last words I said to you were "ok"
On the other side of that "ok" was a "let go"
A moving on, to a new song
The lightest feather blowing through the trees
My mind and heart used to fall to its knees-
To make sure you were ok
But when I needed you
You were not there
When I needed you- all you gave me were selfish
responses baited with care
I needed you
And for all the moments I gave you all of me
Without hesitation or reservation
I wanted to cash in on my deposit
When I needed you
And you weren't there
So here's to saying "ok"
And moving on with my heart under repair

The Climb

We need to cease not having more conversations
about love
We should reach far beyond ourselves to become
givers at the fullest extent
The intent is possible
See when you reach
I'll climb
When you touch
I'll hold
When you fall
I won't fold
There's no difference between us two
As we indulge in purpose
Life can only get better
As we climb...
Together

Still

The girl in the sun still dreams
She still smiles
She's been broken
But healed
Disappointed
But still here
Embracing her power and beauty
Loving herself through every imperfection
Digging deep
Reaching to constantly evolve
The girl in the sun still lives
And still stands tall 🌟

I Miss You

I miss you
Not just the thought of you
But how we used to gleam and dance through
the night of good music
I miss you
Not just the ordinary "hello" or "how's your day"
But the light of your presence
The calm in your voice
The closeness of your body
That took away outside noise
I remember how I leaned into you
Without worry or fret
I have no regrets
And sometimes in my own little corner a smile may
appear
As I reflect on the days of old and want you near
I miss you

The Wait

The nature of love will make me wait
Dancing around its effervescent beauty
Love soothes my body
It's dynamic presence
Makes me wait
Have you ever seen colors of love that captivates your soul?
Has love ever filled the spaces in between that make you feel whole?
Imagine the anticipation
That will make you remember
And wait for love

Beyond the Stars

I would love you beyond the stars
Beyond Jupiter and Mars
I would love you
Beyond measure or reasonable doubt
We would glide in life
Protecting each other from the inevitable changes
grooves that shift and take flight
I would love you
Beyond the night
In between things
In between nature and human beings
I would love you
Because the only thing that would be supreme
...is the protection of your heart
Gaining a fresh start
And loving you beyond the stars
That's how much...
I would love to love you

Needed

We all share one commonality
And that's walking each other home
Day by day
Bit by bit
Our lowest moments carry us on to the next
Sometimes there is a glimpse of happiness but then
it's quickly overshadowed by hurt or even—
An overcast of clouds then our minds are unable to
allow better things to come in
You get tired, you wanna give up
But we keep going
Like damaged goods
there is still some good within
I just hope to get to a place to feel seen and heard,
hugged and loved
Because we only get one shot at this
And in the days to come

When life gets hard and I fall short
I need your presence...

Because you are *needed*

The Memory

During a very special time
In a very special place
I loved you and those feelings will never go away
In the back of my mind I think about all the times we explicitly stared into each other's eyes and just smiled
You made my heart feel worthwhile
Just feeling lost in one another
Such a beautiful feeling
The biggest smile
The warmest hug
Someone special to hold on to
Days, hours not even minutes could equate how much happiness I felt
Sometimes I wonder if it's possible to attain those feelings again
I hope the universe has treated you kind
At times it's so hard for me to hide

That I miss you...

Daydreaming, part 1

If we can be so intentional about time and effort
Then why not be intentional about love
Be intentional about choosing to give
Be intentional about how we choose to live
If love is the end goal
Then why does it seem so far-fetched...

Nice Things

I've met some acquaintances
Some pretty peculiar ones that I've even gone on dates with
Some that say "I'm attracted to your light"
although then at times... they try to dim it
Some pretty handsome Aquarians
Some "I love your vibe, you seem so sweet- how did you become single?"
Some "yes love, I would love to mingle and fly high— with you..."
Some "I know you love the Lord. What church do you go to?"
Some "you know you are a unicorn because you are absolutely beautiful."
But they've all failed to tell the truth
The stories are all the same and no one is ever really emotionally available
Struggling to hold themselves accountable
Because today's "high valued man" has a plan—

To lead you nowhere
Some will even ghost you rather than loathe in your presence as a queen
They want to "add you to the team"
But when you know better, you do better

Because we all deserve *nice things*. ♥

Daydreaming, part 2

Sometimes
I turn around and I see you
When I go to bed at night
Sometimes I dream of you
And when I am smiling midday
Sometimes it's about you
But now that love is done
And I can't run— from my feelings
Should I tell you?
A constant game between heart vs brain
I guess I'll just remain— stuck in a daydream about you

Background

There is a background that I'll play for us
It's filled with so many smiles
Rays of sunshine that yield no end
There is a place for us
That feels just right
A mirage of everything you could dream for is within sight
I'm yours, you're mine
It's like paradise
I'm able to dance so freely
give so easily
There's a background painted in love
Within reach
A Queen willing to honor her King at his feet
It's giving peace
It's giving eternity
It's giving a background of you and me

Solitude (pt. 1)

In solitude is where my mind reflects on all the battles
I've had to silently fight
All the tears I've cried
Getting knocked down 10 times only to get up 10 more
I sit in solitude and think about how I've gotten stronger, how I've managed to show a smile to keep going
There is power in the struggle
Life lessons written in them too
Nothing comes easy but it's all worth it
If you find yourself in solitude
Lean into it, embrace it
Because despite it all...

Dreams do come true

Solitude (pt. 2)

They say solitude brings peace
They say it can bring happiness
Instead I'm stuck in the confines of me
I still dream at night when the stars come out
But the dreams haven't been as bright
My heart is still on the mend
And while the universe brings so much light
My thoughts trace back to you
I wonder if you can feel it too
I remember peace
I remember happiness
At night, in my solitude– is when I remember being with you

Undertaking Love

No matter what anyone ever thinks...
Love will lead the way
True love will captivate your inner soul, your thoughts, your destiny
Real love will be with you on your hardest days and be the very vessel you can depend on
Pure love will serve you, challenge you and be an experience of a lifetime
Don't lose out of love, even if it doesn't come perfectly packaged...
Don't give up on love

Because love will never give up on you.

The Reach

I aligned with you in the clouds
Outside of my reach
The thought of you brought me so much joy
Sweet lasting memories
The times we shared were notably worthwhile
A heart filled with smiles
Love lived there
As my mind turns a page
Out of nowhere...
I suddenly remember the hurt
The moment of abandonment
The abrupt landing and detachment- that struck me deeper than I could have ever imagined
Maybe I dreamed too big
Maybe you always lived... outside of my reach

Tomorrow

I have lots of plans for tomorrow
And I hope you will be there
To hold me, to love me
To be the purest form of eternity
And if we only have just a few moments together
I hope you remember me
Just like a delicacy
Just as refreshing as water
Good for your soul
Just as the sun
That makes you feel whole
I have lots of plans for tomorrow
And I hope you'll be there as we both watch them unfold...

Blooming

Ever seen a flower bloom then decline?
Ever seen someone smile when they make it on the other side?
I see myself dancing in the moonlight
Unattached, healed and free
I see a new bloom, a new me
I revel in her, love and cherish her smile
It's definitely been awhile
But she's here
Beaming with rays from the sun
And still blooming
Her new chapter has just begun

Fresh Start, v. 1

There is a star for me and you
I've managed to move on, in spite of it all,
I really do miss you
I wish the universe led a runway for us
Because the world can be so cold
I remember feeling so warm next to you
I remember the days of old
I keep most things bottled up inside
Because you still reside in a special place in my mind
and in my heart
We are soulmates living apart
So much time has passed
And it's been really hard to grasp
Finding my fresh start

Fresh Start, v. 2

I'm giving up on love
It doesn't feel light like a dove—anymore
Instead what I thought I would give and ultimately
receive feels like constant waves of let downs and
disappointments
Treading like water up against a wall
Love hasn't evolved
Instead I see empty tomorrows
Drifted memories and feelings
I see myself sitting by the water-alone
Without a home for my heart
I'm saying goodbye to love
And will have to continue to figure it out
Maybe I'll find a fresh start
In time and all on my own.

Moving On

We move on
We move on in ways and phrases that the human language cannot understand
We learn
And although it feels like life is weighing us down by the minute at times— we grow
We learn to exude perfection
We learn the value of human relationships
We appreciate the depths of experiences and existence
Life is a constant battle of life thoughts, dreams and aspirations
Finding peace
Finding love
Are all we need to move forward
Believe in yourself because...
There's so much more greatness to come

Daydreaming, part 3

Someone once asked, "What do you want to do for the rest of your life?"

My response is...

"I just want to live in the sun, write and be alone in my dreams."

The Wait

The nature of love will make me wait
Dancing around its effervescent beauty
Love soothes my body
It's dynamic presence
Makes me wait
Have you ever seen colors of love that captivates your soul?
Has love ever filled the spaces in between that make you feel whole?
Imagine the anticipation
That will make you remember
And wait for love

The Colors of Love

The colors of love looks like pure skies and sun
Sweet conversations
Some go undone
Long hugs
Whispers in the ear
Two resting spirits
Who always want to be near
A moment where my wildest dreams come true
The colors of love represent you
Soft moments you can always recall
Lost in time is where we evolve
Like the clear blue ocean
The sunset that takes our breath away
In my mind is where you will always stay
Because the colors will always remain true
The color of love is you. ♥

Paradise

If love doesn't make you jump out of your seat and
run towards it– then are you truly excited?
If hearing a person's name doesn't ignite the flame in
your heart– are you truly meant to grow together or
ease apart?
I see you, I see me
I can see the sun—a gentle pleasantry
Such encounters happen maybe once or twice in life–
an easy setting where it feels like paradise.
The ability to laugh, to be free, a devoted connection–
chemistry
Maybe once or twice in life–
go after it, follow your heart
or you just might miss...

Paradise

Remembering You

On a rainy night, where do your thoughts lie?
Mine lie with you
As the rain drops make a sound
I can remember being around—you
Some say, when it rains, it pours
Well I remember when I used to adore—you
The lightness in your eyes
The gentle spirit you tried to hide
Your vulnerability was so true
We used to laugh
We used to dream
We used to discuss all kinds of things
No matter the weather
The rain brought us together
And I remember you. ♥

Good Love

If love is an emotional feeling
Then why do we run from it?
If you can see the person within reach that you want
to spend the rest of your life with–
Then why don't we run towards it?
To live in total bliss seems like just a myth
Instead we place fear over practice
Hide our heart behind the "what ifs"
Instead of exuding vulnerability
Before you run
Think about taking the risk
And reflect on...
How good love once felt to you...

To all of my dreamers...
Keep going, Keep loving,
Keep believing...
Again, thank you for
dreaming with me.
♡

www.ingramcontent.com/pod-product-compliance
Lightning Source LLC
Chambersburg PA
CBHW072138070526
44585CB00016B/1728